3 9082 07414 7110

D1621582

J
621.366
Par   Parker, Steve

Lasers

Redford Township District Library
25320 West Six Mile Road
Redford, MI 48240

www.redford.lib.mi.us

Hours:

Mon-Thur 10-8:30
Fri-Sat 10-5
Sunday (School Year) 12-5

NO LONGER
THE PROPERTY OF
RTDL

REDFORD TWP DISTRICT LIBRARY

FEB 1 8 2004

LASERS

NOW AND INTO THE FUTURE

Steve Parker

ILLUSTRATED BY INDUSTRIAL ART STUDIO

Thameside Press

US publication copyright © 2002 Thameside Press
International copyright reserved in all countries.
No part of this book may be reproduced in any form
without writtten permission from the publisher.

Distributed in the United States by
Smart Apple Media
1980 Lookout Drive
North Mankato, MN 56003

Text copyright © Steve Parker 1998

Series editor Veronica Ross
Editor Julie Hill
Designer Hayley Cove
Design Assistant Rachel Ludbrook
Illustrations by Industrial Art Studio
Production Raj Trivedi
Consultants Ian Graham and Virginia Whitby
Picture researcher Diana Morris

ISBN 1-931983-24-0
Library of Congress Control Number XXXX

3 9082 07414 7110

Printed by South China Printing Co. Ltd., Hong Kong

Photo credits
t=top; b=bottom; c=center; l=left; r=right
Belitha Press: 27l photo Claire Paxton.
Berenguier/Jerrican/SPL: 4–5.
Custom Medical Stock/SPL: 10c.
Eddy Gray/SPL: 17b.
Adam Hart-Davis/SPL: 21c.
Phillip Hayson/SPL: 18c. Tim Hazael/SPL: 19b.
Robert Holmgren/SPL: 12c. Jerrican/SPL: 28.
Manfred Kage/SPL: 17t. Peter Menzell/SPL: 6c.
M. Astrid & Hans Frieder Michler/SPL: 16t.
NASA/SPL: 21t, 26b.
Odile Noel/Redferns: 14c.
Philippe Plailly/SPL: 22b, 23b.
Rosenfeld Images/SPL: 13t.
Paul Shambroom/SPL: 4.
Stockmarket/Zefa: 5t.
Alexander Tsiaras/SPL: 10b, 26t, 29.
Geoff Tompkinson/SPL: 24t.
© Twentieth Century Fox/Kobal Collection: 25t.
US Dept. of Defence/SPL: 24b.

Words in **bold** appear in the Glossary on pages 30-31.

CONTENTS

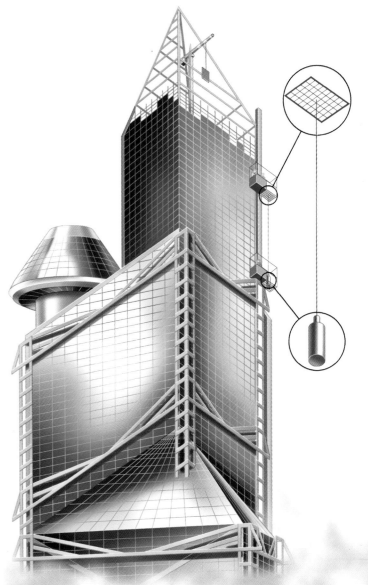

In May 1960, American scientist Theodore Maiman produced the world's first laser beam, a **pulse** of bright red light. This was the beginning of a huge new industry, developing lasers and putting them to hundreds, even thousands, of uses in science, technology, arts, and entertainment.

LASERS IN ACTION

Today there are at least a hundred different kinds of lasers—found in all sorts of equipment. Laser light can carry phone calls, play CDs in music systems, and read information on computer CD-ROMs. Lasers are also used in surgery. **Laser scalpels** make very fine cuts that reduce bleeding during operations. Lasers can also be used to drill teeth painlessly.

Laser light is used to scan information on bar codes at store checkouts, factories, and warehouses.

INDUSTRIAL USES

Lasers are used in industry to cut and **weld** strong metals. They can measure distances accurately, so they are used in engineering projects to build bridges, railroads, and tunnels. Lasers are also used in **fiber-optic** cables for **telecommunications**, to guide missiles, and to make holograms. The list of their uses goes on and on.

 Lasers are accurate measuring tools that are used for large building projects, such as bridges.

 Shaped pieces of cloth are cut accurately by laser beams and joined to make clothes.

OUT OF SIGHT

Lasers are usually hidden inside equipment so that we cannot see them. But we can see the amazing laser beams that are used in spectacular light displays at big concerts and stage shows. Most people never see a laser working. This is partly because laser light can be very powerful. If it shines into our eyes, it may damage them, and may even cause blindness. Special safety precautions are needed when using strong lasers. They are known by their users as "eyeball-poppers" because, if the worst happens, that's exactly what they do.

▶ FUTURE TREND

Predicting the future is very difficult. A new invention may be in daily use in five years time, or it may be delayed for 30 years. It may never happen at all. What is certain is that technology develops all the time. *Future Trend* looks at new developments, which may happen in 20, 40, or even 60 years. They may seem impossible to us today. But for people 60 years ago, so did lasers.

LIGHT AND LASER LIGHT

Light from the sun, a candle, or an electric lamp brightens our world. Ordinary light and laser light are similar in some ways, but different in others. They are different in three main ways—in their color, **coherence**, and spread.

COLORS OF THE RAINBOW

Ordinary white light, such as natural light or light from an electric lamp, is made up of many different colors of light, all with different **wavelengths**. The color of light depends on the length of its waves. Longer **light waves** are red and orange, medium ones are yellow and green, and shorter light waves are blue, indigo, and violet. These are the colors of the rainbow. Mix them together, and they make ordinary white light.

 When it rains on a sunny day, we often see the colors of light appear in the sky—as a rainbow.

THE SPEED OF LIGHT

All kinds of light, including laser and natural light, travel very fast—at about 186,000 miles per second. This seems incredibly fast to us, but distances in space are huge. The sun is almost 93 million miles from Earth, and its light takes over eight minutes to reach us.

▶ ALL ABOUT LIGHT

Laser light, like ordinary white light, travels in a straight line. But mirrors and **lenses** can be used to direct and **focus** laser light in the same way as ordinary light. Mirrors reflect light. A laser beam can be reflected by mirrors and directed to a certain spot. Laser light can be bent in the same way as ordinary light. This is called **refraction**. Lenses are used to refract light—to bend rays and change their direction. You can read more about reflection and refraction later in this book.

▶ FUTURE TREND

LISTENING TO AN ANT'S FOOTSTEPS? Lasers amplify, or strengthen, light waves to produce an incredibly powerful beam of light. Might it be possible to strengthen sound waves in a similar way, by a "saser"? The saser could pick up the tiniest sounds, like an ant's footsteps, and strengthen them into deafening booms. It could also be used in music systems to bring the sound of a huge rock concert into your living room. Be careful of your eardrums!

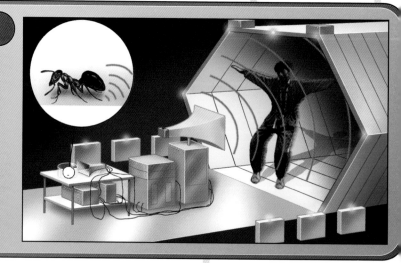

COLOR

White light is made up of many different colors—all with different wavelengths. But laser light is one pure color, and all its waves are exactly the same length. The color depends mainly on the substance the laser is made from. This is called the **active medium**. For example, the beam from a ruby laser is red, because the active medium is mainly the precious red gem, ruby.

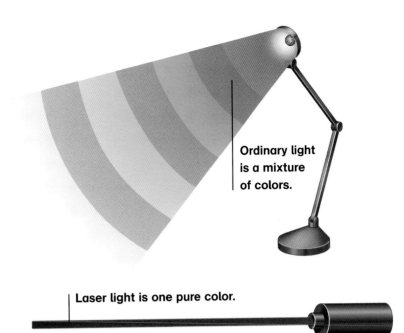

Ordinary light is a mixture of colors.

Laser light is one pure color.

Ordinary light waves are not in step.

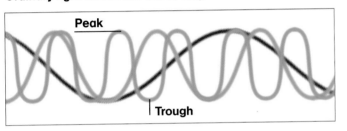

Peak

Trough

Laser light waves are in step.

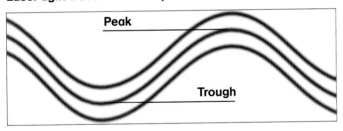

Peak

Trough

SPREAD

Ordinary light waves spread out from their source, becoming farther apart. So a narrow beam of ordinary light, even the most powerful spotlight, spreads out and eventually fades. Laser light waves do not spread. They are parallel, which means that they are the same distance apart. A beam from a laser stays the same width even if it travels to the moon and back. These three features of pure color, coherence, and spread give lasers their great power and usefulness.

COHERENCE

In ordinary light the peaks (highest parts) and troughs (lowest parts) of the different waves are not in line. The waves go up and down, but they are out of step with each other. Laser light has all its peaks and troughs exactly lined up with each other. This is called coherence. It gives laser light more strength, so it travels much farther without fading.

Ordinary light waves spread from their source.

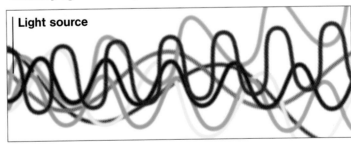

Light source

Laser light waves remain parallel.

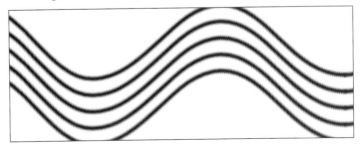

HOW LASERS WORK

Most lasers work like a special kind of flashlight. Inside a laser a beam of light is strengthened by energy that is "pumped" in. The beam that comes out is an incredibly powerful pulse of light. The word *laser* means Light Amplification by **Stimulated Emission** of **Radiation**, and this describes what happens inside a laser. A typical laser has three main parts—an active medium, an energy source, and reflectors—which work together to produce a laser beam.

INSIDE A RUBY LASER

The energy source is a coiled flash tube. It gives out energy as powerful pulses of light. This energy works on the active medium.

The active medium is the gem, ruby. It consists of tiny particles, called **atoms**, which absorb energy from the energy source.

Energy source

Total reflector

Active medium

ATOMS AT WORK

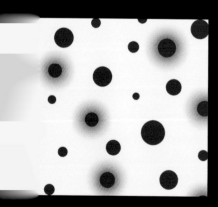

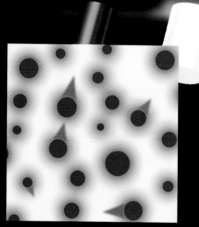

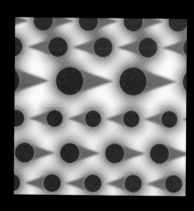

Inside the ruby rod, light energy from the energy source hits the atoms. Some of them take in this energy and become excited. They begin to give off their own light energy.

4 The light energy given off by an excited atom hits a nearby atom that is already excited. This stimulates the second atom to give out an identical flash of light or photon. This is called stimulated emission.

5 Stimulated emission produces more and more photons that bounce back and forth off the reflecting surfaces at opposite ends of the ruby rod. This is when lasing begins.

LIGHT AND OTHER RAYS

Light rays or waves are a type of energy called electromagnetic energy. They shine out, or radiate, from their source, so they are called electromagnetic radiation. Light rays are just a tiny part of a huge range of rays and waves called the electromagnetic spectrum (EMS).

The parts of the electromagnetic spectrum have different wavelengths and different names.

| Radio waves | Microwaves | Infrared waves | Light waves | Ultraviolet waves | X-rays | Gamma rays |

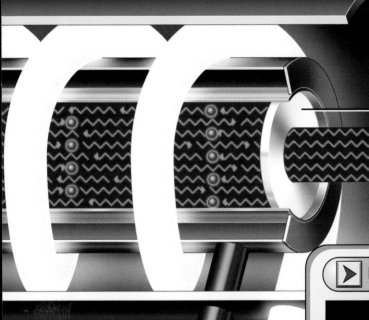

Partial reflector

Laser beam

MAKING A LASER BEAM

6 The laser is pumped, or powered, by light energy from the flash tube. The light is being increased, or amplified.

7 The light bouncing back and forth inside the rod becomes so powerful that some of it passes through the partial reflector and emerges as a laser beam.

▶ FUTURE TREND

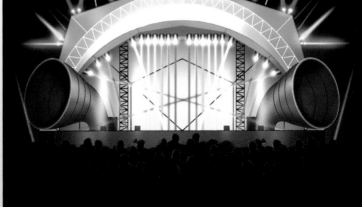

SHOUT AT THE LASER?
Lasers can be "pumped" by almost any kind of energy, including light, electricity, chemical changes, **nuclear** power, or even by another laser. Sound is also a form of energy. Perhaps there will be a sound-pumped laser that needs no electricity or switch. Simply shout at it, and it gives out a flash of laser light. But to make a continually shining beam would make your throat sore!

LIFESAVING LASERS

Lasers were used in medicine almost as soon as they were invented. In traditional surgery a very sharp knife called a scalpel is used to cut into body **tissues**. But now surgeons can use laser scalpels to perform some operations. A laser scalpel makes a very fine cut with a laser beam. Its beam is so focused that it can be used for very delicate surgery, such as on the eye or brain.

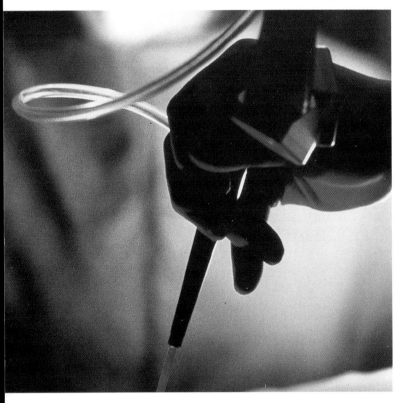

SKIN-DEEP

More than a dozen types of lasers are now used in medicine. One type of laser scalpel uses the gas carbon dioxide as its active medium. As the laser cuts, the heat seals the tiny **blood vessels**. This means that the cut bleeds less. An argon laser, with the gas argon as the active medium, produces a beam that can remove certain kinds of birthmarks.

BORING THROUGH BONE

A xenon, or YAG, laser **vaporizes** solid bone to bore through the skull to the brain. Laser light can also shine along a fiber-optic tube, or **endoscope**, inserted into the body. The laser beam cuts or welds tissue, seals ulcers, destroys blood clots, and carries out other treatments deep inside the body.

A surgeon's gloved hand holds a laser scalpel during an operation. The beam is switched on to cut and off for safety.

An argon laser is being used here to treat throat cancer. The beam kills the cancerous growths, called tumors.

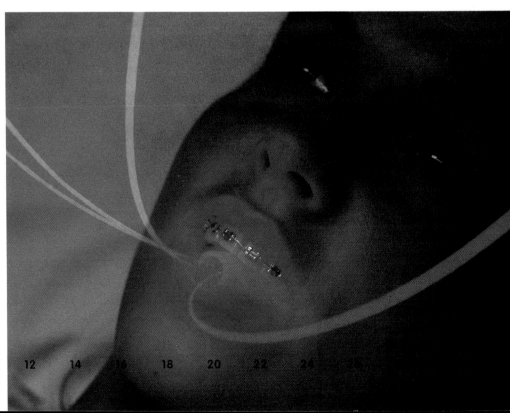

IMPROVING EYESIGHT

Some people with poor eyesight can have laser treatment to improve their vision. A laser beam shines at the eye and heats away part of the cornea–the domed front part of the eye. Reshaping the cornea in this way may mean that people no longer have to wear glasses or contact lenses.

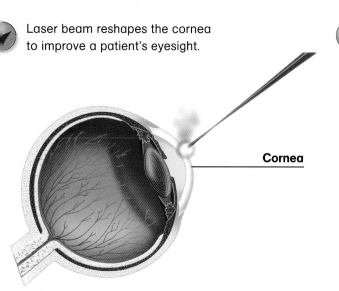

Laser beam reshapes the cornea to improve a patient's eyesight.

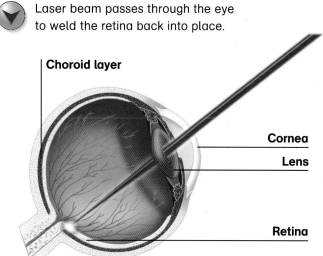

Laser beam passes through the eye to weld the retina back into place.

Choroid layer

Cornea

Lens

Retina

FOCUSING A LASER

A laser beam can be finely focused to concentrate its energy at an accurate distance from the laser's tip. This means that the laser light can pass through the surface of the body without harming it, and cut or heat-weld the parts where it is focused. This is how some laser eye surgery works.

EYE SURGERY

The retina is the light-sensitive layer at the back of the eye. It may become detached from the choroid layer of the eye, resulting in loss of sight. A laser beam can be used to mend a detached retina. The beam passes into the eye and is focused by the eye's lens onto the retina. It then welds the retina back into place without harming the rest of the eye.

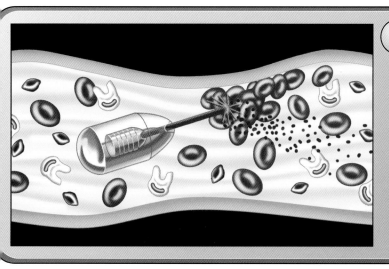

▶ FUTURE TREND

THE NANOSURGEON?
Nanotechnology is the science of incredibly small machines (see page 17). Some are even smaller than the microscopic cells that make up the human body. Lasers are getting smaller, too. In the future a nanomachine with a nanolaser could be injected into the body. It could travel around in the blood vessels, zap a troublesome blood clot with laser light, and then dissolve itself into small, harmless pieces.

LASERS IN INDUSTRY

Scientists continue to develop more powerful lasers in which the laser beam is concentrated into a spot of powerful energy. This has made lasers very useful in heavy industry, particularly in working with hard, strong metals.

SQUARE HOLES

The high power of a focused laser can heat and melt materials, such as steel, and burn right through them. It can even drill square holes! A laser beam doesn't have a cutting edge that needs sharpening like a saw, and it leaves fewer sharp edges and dribbles of **molten** metal. The laser beam simply turns the metal into a vapor that drifts away.

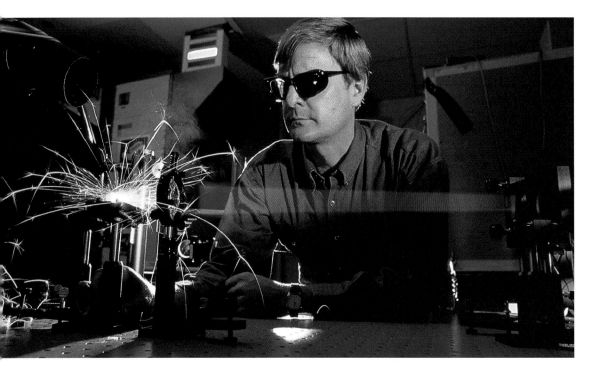

 A laser beam cutting through metal. Technicians wear goggles to protect their eyes from the laser light.

▶ FUTURE TREND

UNLIMITED POWER?
One pulse of light from an American research laser was 1,300 times more powerful than the country's entire electricity system. But this burst of energy lasted only one-half of one-millionth of one-millionth of a second. If lasers could flash energy, such as light, across long distances, perhaps receivers could turn it into electricity. Then there would be no need for electricity cables crisscrossing the land.

CONTROLLED BY COMPUTERS

The laser beam's energy is focused into such a tiny place that its heat does not spread through the material. This produces less damage near the cut. Computers control the movement of the laser or the material for exact cutting and trimming. Lasers can also make very accurate spot welds. Two pieces of metal are heated and melt together over a very small area. It's like joining them with tiny dabs of ultrastrong glue.

Lasers are used to make complicated machinery, such as this part for a power plant.

HARD METAL

Industrial researchers are developing stronger metals and materials all the time to make jet engines, high-speed **bearings**, and other machine parts. The problem is, the harder the materials, the more difficult they are to cut, trim, smooth, and polish, because other materials are too soft. Once again the answer is a laser.

A low-power laser shines, reflects, and refracts to check that the faces of the diamond are at equal angles.

A high-power laser bores a hole right through a diamond to cut a particular shape.

A medium-power laser shaves off the diamond's rough edges to make the faces smooth.

TOUGH DIAMONDS

A diamond is the hardest natural substance on Earth. When dug from the ground, it is a rough-looking lump, which must be cut, shaped, and polished to make a beautiful jewel. One way of doing this is to use cutting tools tipped with smaller, less valuable diamonds, because only other diamonds are hard enough. An alternative is to use a laser. Some laser beams are so powerful that they can drill right through a diamond.

One of the few times that people see laser beams is at a big event, such as a concert or a sports display. The multi-colored, pencil-thin beams spread out and crisscross high above, moving in patterns in time with the music.

LASER LIGHT SHOWS

Laser light shows are very strictly controlled. Powerful laser beams must never shine down into the audience, since they could harm a viewer's eyes. They must always point upward or where there are no people. Some laser light is quite weak, so it cannot harm viewers even if it does shine in their eyes for a short time. But weaker beams are duller and much less spectacular.

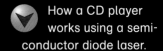

How a CD player works using a semi-conductor diode laser.

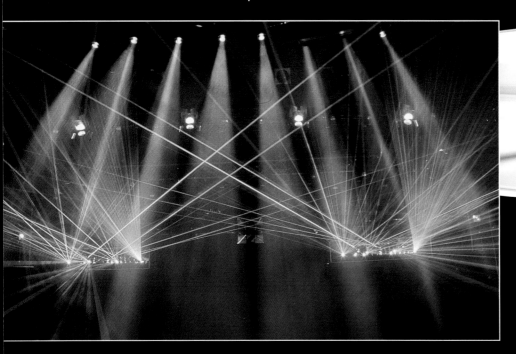

A spectacular laser light show adds to the excitement of a pop concert.

MOVING BEAMS

Laser light reflects off mirrors, just like ordinary light. In a laser light show, the beams move by shining on mirrors, which are tilted by computer-controlled motors, to reflect them at different angles. The different colors are made either by using different types of lasers, or by passing the beams through tinted **filters**.

Turntable motor ——————

A MINIATURE LASER

The most common type of laser is a **semiconductor** diode laser. It is about as big as a grain of rice. In its tiny case it is small enough to sit on a fingernail. The laser is made from a thin slice of a substance called a semiconductor–the same material that is used in computer **microchips**. The laser is pumped by electricity, and the beam comes out of the end. This is the device used in CD players, CD-ROM computer drives, videodisc players, computer laser printers, and **image scanners**.

▶ **FUTURE TREND**

YOUR WORLD ON CD?
A typical CD, read by laser light, holds 75 minutes of music, 100 million words, or one minute of high-quality video film. Already the next generation of discs, DVD (digital versatile discs), hold 15 or 30 times more information. Where will it end? One day a single CD might hold all the words, sounds, and pictures you've ever experienced. Your life on disc!

Compact disc (CD)

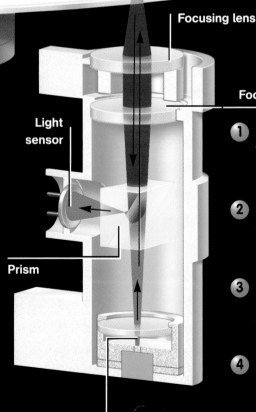

Focusing lens

Focusing lens

Light sensor

Prism

Laser

1 Laser beam passes through prism and up to disc.

2 Laser beam reflects off disc and back down to prism.

3 Laser beam passes into prism and out to light sensor.

4 Light sensor turns reflected light into electrical signals for the CD player.

▶ READING A CD

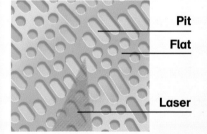

Pit

Flat

Laser

Laser beams are used to detect the information stored on a CD. A tiny red laser beam passes through a **prism** and focuses through a lens onto the CD. The disc's shiny surface has billions of microscopic **pits**, in a pattern that represents coded information, such as music or a computer program. As the disc spins, the beam reflects off the flat parts of the disc, but not off the pits. The patterns of reflected light shine back through the prism and onto a light **sensor**, which turns them into electrical signals.

MADE BY MICRO-LASER

Powerful industrial lasers can cut and weld tough materials, such as steel. But much smaller lasers—micro-lasers—also have their uses, such as drilling tiny holes, or shaving off almost invisible layers of material. These jobs would be difficult, if not impossible, with other tools.

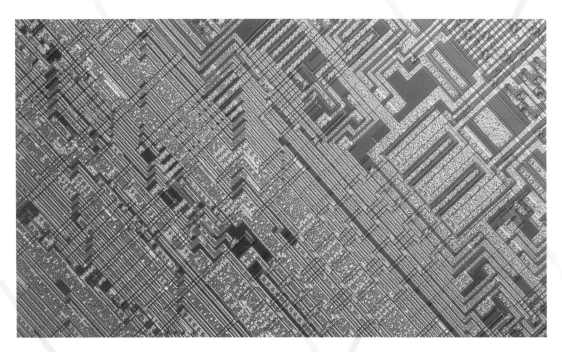

An enlarged view of an integrated circuit, or microchip. This shows clearly the millions of components on the chip.

MAKING MICROCHIPS

Lasers are used to make **integrated circuits**, or microchips, which are used in computers. The laser beam, a hundred times thinner than a human hair, shines back and forth at a thin slice, or "chip," of the semiconductor **silicon**. It removes the surface of the silicon to leave a pattern of millions of **electronic components** and **microcircuits**.

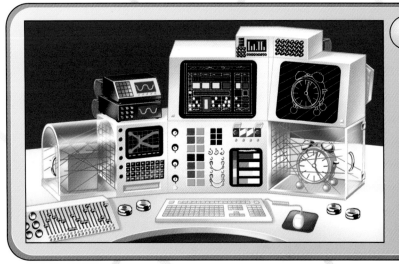

▶ FUTURE TREND

FACTORY ON A DESKTOP?
Desktop publishing is now common. Typesetting machines and printing presses, which used to fill a room, have been replaced by computers and printers that fit on a desk. Could factories be the same? You could feed a lump of all-purpose raw material into a machine. Lasers would cut, mold, shape, and join it into dozens of parts. From the same material, but with different control programs, a desktop factory could produce anything from a clock to a computer.

The gears, wheels, and motors of micro-machines are ultra tiny, as shown here next to a fly's leg! Lasers also shape smaller mechanical parts, called nanomachines.

Under a microscope, germs can be moved, separated, and studied using laser beams.

NANOMACHINES

The growing science of nanotechnology deals with machines and devices that are nano, which is even smaller than micro (see page 11). Hundreds of nanomachines, such as wheels, drills, gears, and even motors, could fit onto the period at the end of this sentence. Lasers are used to make these tiny machines by welding, melting, and turning any unwanted solid parts into a vapor.

TWEEZERS OF LIGHT

A laser beam shining down a microscope can be used like a pair of **optical** tweezers. The beam is focused onto an incredibly tiny object, such as a germ or a single cell. The concentrated energy of the beam can hold the cell or germ still or move it around, as though it were gripped by a pair of real tweezers.

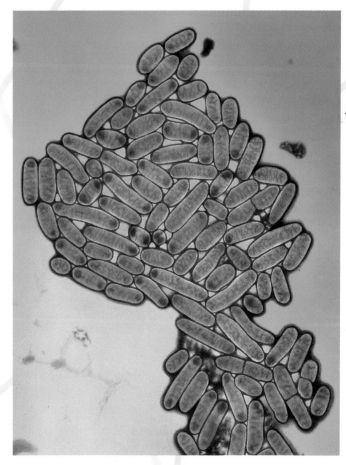

TALKING BY LASER

Telephones work by electricity. The mouthpiece picks up the sound of your voice and changes it into a pattern of electrical signals. These go along metal wires to another telephone, where the earpiece turns them back into sound waves. But all this is changing, and lasers are the key.

FLASHES OF LIGHT

In a long wire, electrical signals become **distorted** and fade away. So most long-distance telephone cables now work by laser light. The cable is a bundle of thousands of optical fibers, or fiber optics. Each fiber is a long, thin, bendable rod or strand of special clear glass, thinner than a hair. It carries flashes of laser light. The pattern of flashes represents information, such as the sound of your voice. The flashes change back into electrical signals for the local telephone network.

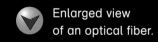

Enlarged view of an optical fiber.

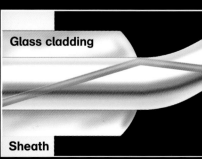

Glass cladding

Sheath

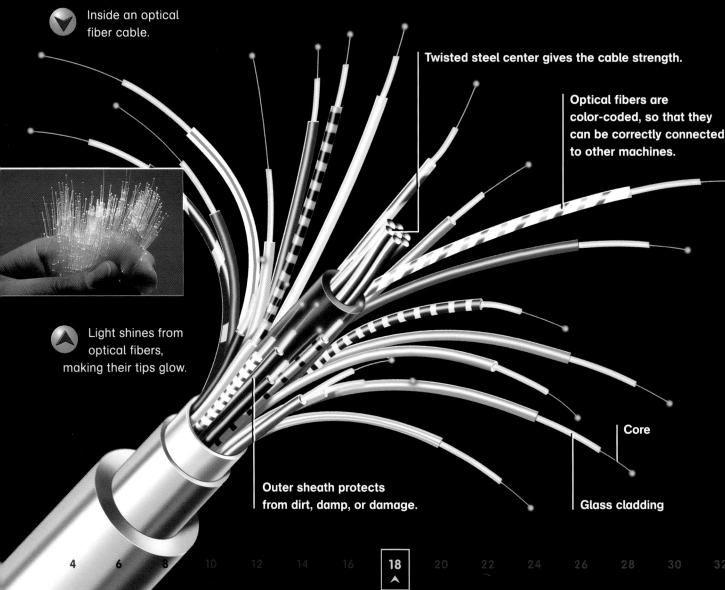

Inside an optical fiber cable.

Twisted steel center gives the cable strength.

Optical fibers are color-coded, so that they can be correctly connected to other machines.

Light shines from optical fibers, making their tips glow.

Core

Outer sheath protects from dirt, damp, or damage.

Glass cladding

ZIGZAGGING LASERS

Laser light travels in straight lines. But optical fibers can be bent, and laser light will still travel through them. Inside the fiber the laser beam bounces or reflects off the inner surface. This is called internal reflection. So the laser beam zigzags along the fiber—even if the fiber is bent. This is how optical fibers carry laser light signals around curves and corners.

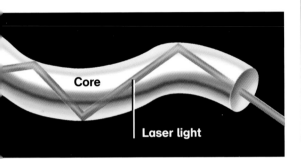

Core

Laser light

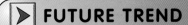

▶ FUTURE TREND

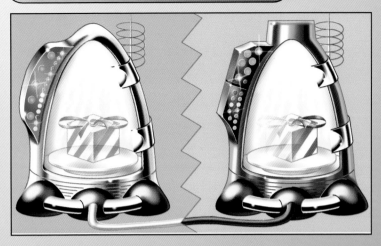

EVERYTHING BY CABLE?
Laser light pulses in optical fiber cables already bring us phone calls, music, TV channels, movies, computer data, information from banks, and much, much more. Could there be a light-into-substance transporter device that changes laser signals into real objects? It could produce food, drink, clothes, even friends from the end of the cable.

BETTER THAN ELECTRICITY

The latest lasers switch on and off hundreds of millions of times each second—that's a lot of flashes. Optical fibers carry information at least 100 times faster than the metal wires that carry electricity. This information could be the sound of your voice or signals from a fax machine or computer, and could represent words, pictures, sounds, computer programs, and almost anything else.

▶ SENDING SIGNALS FARTHER

Laser light signals go much farther than electrical signals, but they, too, eventually fade. They need to be boosted or strengthened regularly. To do this, a different type of laser light shines along the length of the optical fiber, and pumps it with energy. This energy then transfers itself to the coded pulses of laser light, strengthening them as they go. Using this system, laser signals could go ten times around the earth without fading —if there was a fiber long enough.

The telecommunications network of phones, computers, and other machines uses laser light in optical cables.

MEASURING BY LASER

A laser beam makes a perfectly straight-edged and very long ruler. Laser beams are used to line up large structures, such as skyscrapers, bridges, and railroad lines, as they are being built, to make sure they are completely straight.

GOING STRAIGHT

Light travels very fast in a straight line. Laser light is particularly good for judging straight lines, because it is so focused and does not spread out, even over huge distances (see page 7).

THE LASER TAPE MEASURE

It is also possible to measure distances accurately using a laser. Send off a very short pulse of laser light, one-millionth of a second long. It bounces off a mirror and comes back a fraction of a second later. If you measure the time it takes and multiply it by the speed of light, you can work out the distance to the mirror and back. This makes lasers the longest and most accurate tape measures in the world.

Laser beams are ideal for aligning, or lining up, the parts of big structures, such as skyscrapers.

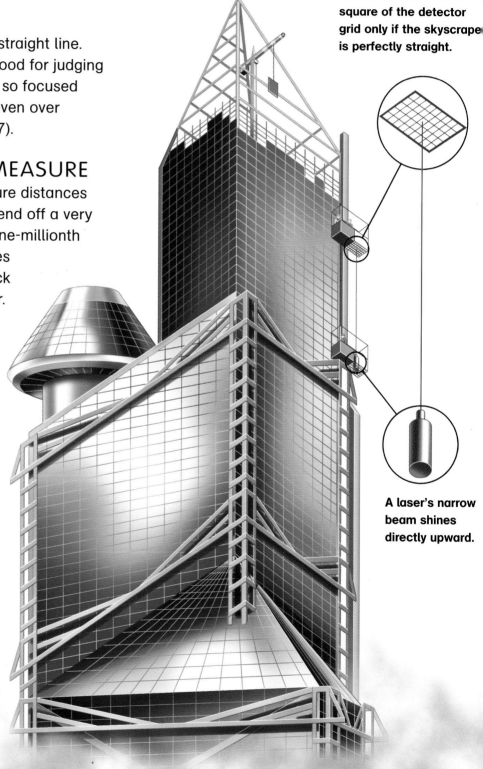

The beam hits the central square of the detector grid only if the skyscraper is perfectly straight.

A laser's narrow beam shines directly upward.

FROM EARTH TO SPACE

Laser tape measures can easily tell the distance from the top of one mountain to the next. Lasers can also shine up to satellites in space to see

how high they are, or measure the distance to the moon. Laser beams are bounced back to Earth off laser reflectors like this one on the moon, to give an accurate distance.

SHIFTING CONTINENTS

Laser measurements show that the earth's surface is constantly changing. Volcanoes grow taller, earthquakes split the land, and the continents drift slowly around the globe. They only move by a few inches each year, but lasers can detect these movements.

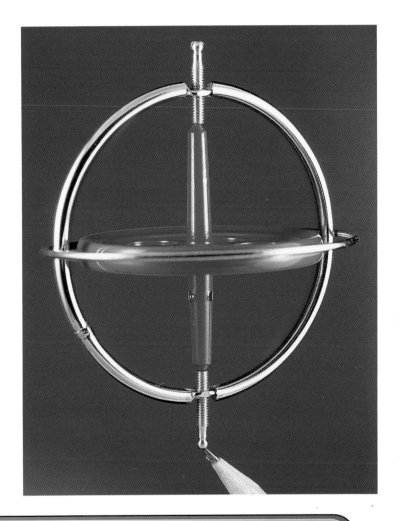

STAYING STEADY

A gyroscope is a heavy wheel that spins on its **axle**. It is set into a framework of joints and bearings, so that it can swivel and tilt. It tends to stay steady, in the same position, as things around it move. Gyroscopes are used in most big planes, ships, submarines, missiles, rockets, satellites, and spacecraft, to help measure speed and position and to keep them steady. New laser gyroscopes are much more accurate and have hardly any moving parts. They could make all kinds of travel and navigation much safer.

A fast-spinning gyroscope stays steady and balances even on the tip of a pencil.

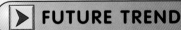

▶ FUTURE TREND

GOLD IN THE BACK YARD?

Laser light reflects off any natural shiny surface, such as rocks, water, or pools of oil or tar. The way the light is scattered or changed shows the type of surface in great detail. So laser beams are used to detect certain kinds of rocks, which might contain valuable substances, such as gold, oil, or diamonds. Could you strike it lucky and get rich quick?

LASER HOLOGRAMS

Have you ever seen a hologram? It's a picture, for example, a face. Like an ordinary picture it has width and height. But a hologram also has depth. As you move around it, you can see the sides or top of the face, and even behind it. Like a real face the hologram is in 3D (three dimensions)–up-down, side-side, front-back. But it is on a flat surface, with only two dimensions.

MADE BY LASER

Holograms are made using laser light. There are two main types of holograms–a transmission hologram and a reflection hologram–and they are made in different ways. The diagram shows how a reflection hologram is made.

1 A laser shines at a part-silvered mirror. This lets some light through to form the object beam, and reflects the rest to form the reference beam.

Ruby laser

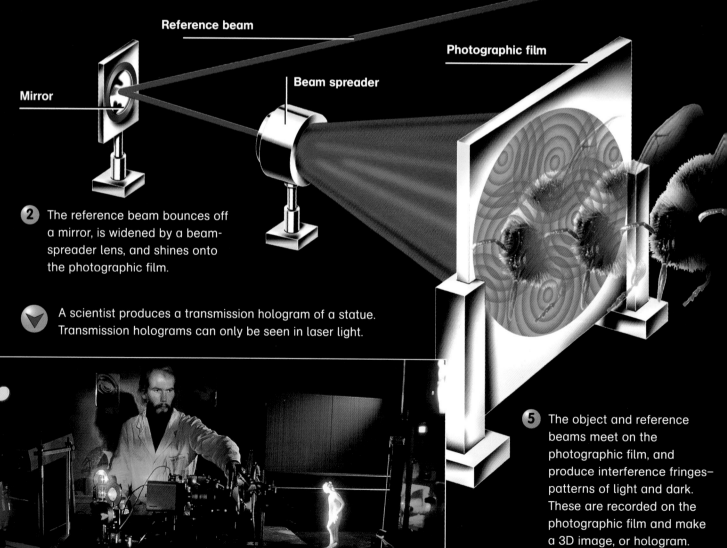

Reference beam

Photographic film

Mirror

Beam spreader

2 The reference beam bounces off a mirror, is widened by a beam-spreader lens, and shines onto the photographic film.

A scientist produces a transmission hologram of a statue. Transmission holograms can only be seen in laser light.

5 The object and reference beams meet on the photographic film, and produce interference fringes–patterns of light and dark. These are recorded on the photographic film and make a 3D image, or hologram.

▶ FUTURE TREND

HOLOGRAM MEMORIES?

Computer holographic memories, in 3D, could store much more than 2D memory devices, such as CDs. Crisscrossing laser beams produce coded patterns of tiny dark spots inside a special crystal, like a 3D crossword puzzle. This could represent the full 3D appearance of a room or building—even of an ancient city or castle—in an object smaller than a sugar cube. Lasers shining into the cube could create a full-sized 3D view, like a giant hologram.

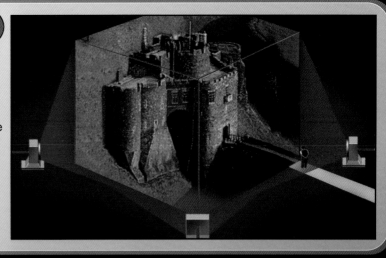

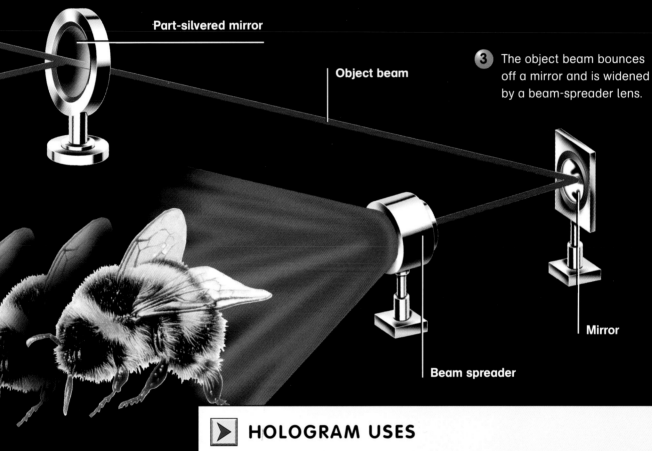

Part-silvered mirror

Object beam

3 The object beam bounces off a mirror and is widened by a beam-spreader lens.

Mirror

Beam spreader

4 The beam shines on the object, and is scattered and reflected in a complicated way. These scattered reflections shine onto the photographic film.

▶ HOLOGRAM USES

▶ As eye-catching covers for books, magazines, and badges.

▶ 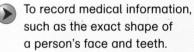 As security signs on credit cards or entrance and exit passes. Holograms are very difficult to forge.

▶ To store complicated 3D information, such as maps of underground train lines or caves.

▶ To record medical information, such as the exact shape of a person's face and teeth.

▶ Computer-generated holograms can show objects in **virtual reality**, without your having to make them. Examples include an architect's model of a skyscraper, or the new design for a car or plane.

▶ To record valuable 3D objects, such as gems, accurately.

LASERS IN WARTIME

Lasers have lots of military uses, and these are growing all the time. Laser beams can light up targets to make attack easier, and laser-guided missiles can be aimed with amazing accuracy.

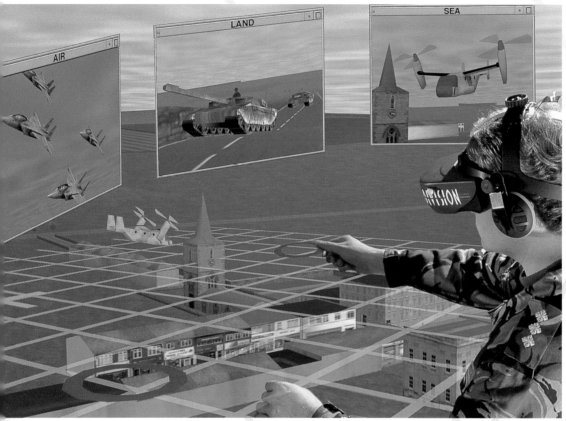

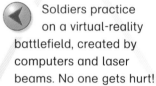

Soldiers practice on a virtual-reality battlefield, created by computers and laser beams. No one gets hurt!

This old space rocket was heated by a powerful test laser and was destroyed when its fuel exploded.

LASER-GUIDED MISSILES

A missile may have a laser-based gyroscope to make it fly in a steady, controlled way (see page 21). A laser range-finder can measure a missile's height above the ground, or the distance to landmarks, such as hills and big buildings. And a laser-guidance system can direct a missile to its target.

ON TARGET

In one type of guidance system, a sensor on the missile detects a laser beam shining at the target from a nearby plane, ship, or even from a satellite in space. The missile locks onto the laser beam and follows it exactly to the target.

Aliens could use laser-powered weapons, as in this scene from the movie *Independence Day*.

▶ SAFER SHOOTING

Lasers can be used for practicing shooting. A special gun can fire very weak, safe pulses of laser light instead of bullets. These bounce off targets, such as mirrors or shiny plastic discs that whiz through the air. The flash of returning light is detected by a sensor on the gun. A flash of light means a direct hit. No flash means you've missed the target.

LASER WEAPONS

The concentrated energy of a laser beam could be used as a fire-starting weapon. If the sun's light and heat shine through a bottle in a forest and focus a tiny hot area onto dry leaves, the leaves sometimes catch fire. This is how forest fires can start. In the same way a high-powered laser could set fire to targets, such as bridges and buildings. It could even start a brush fire to smoke out the enemy. These laser beams could be sent from almost anywhere —from a land vehicle, plane, or missile, or even from a satellite in space.

▶ FUTURE TREND

MELTED BY A HASER?
A laser works with light, which is part of the electromagnetic spectrum, or EMS (see page 9). Another part of the EMS is infrared rays, or heat rays. A "haser" could produce a powerful beam of infrared rays. These would be invisible, but they could melt huge objects, such as icebergs, from many miles away. A haser could also be a very powerful weapon!

MASERS

The first maser was built in 1954, six years before the first laser. A maser is like a laser, but instead of light, it produces a pure and coherent beam of **microwaves**. Microwaves are part of the EMS (see page 9). They are longer than light waves—each wave is several inches long—and, unlike light, they are invisible to the human eye.

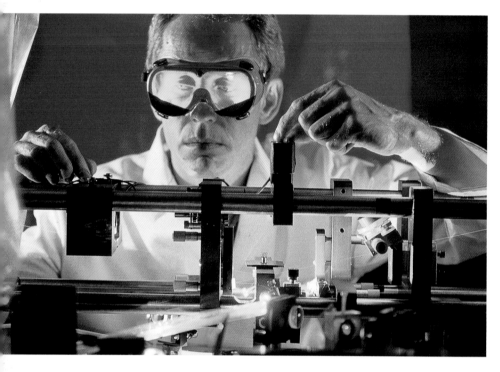

ENERGETIC ATOMS

Masers are mainly used in certain types of atomic clocks. Atomic clocks are the most accurate timekeepers in the world. They tell the time by measuring energy changes in atoms. In a maser-based atomic clock, microwave energy is beamed into a chamber that contains the gas hydrogen. The atoms in the hydrogen take energy from the microwaves and begin to vibrate at an incredible speed—almost one and a half billion times each second.

Some types of atomic clocks work using lasers, such as this dye laser, instead of masers.

ACCURATE TIMEKEEPER

A laser beam detects these vibrations. This means that time can be measured in billionths of a second, far more accurately than a stopwatch, which works in hundredths of a second. If an atomic clock could run for 30 million years, it would lose or gain less than a second.

ECHOES OF THE BIG BANG?

Masers are also used in space research. They detect and amplify, or strengthen, the faint microwaves that continually pass through deep space and hit the earth. These microwaves are probably left-over energy from the **big bang** billions of years ago, when the whole universe, and time itself, began.

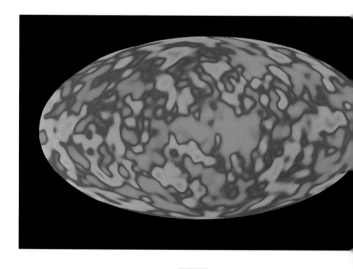

If you could detect microwaves in space, as a maser can, they might look like this.

▶ MORE LASER POWER

The power of a laser is measured in **watts**. An ordinary light bulb can be 60 or 100 watts. Laser light is so strong that just a few milliwatts (thousandths of a watt) shining into the eye can cause blindness. This is why lasers need so many safety precautions. Big industrial lasers produce more than one million watts in an area the size of a fingernail. The biggest lasers planned for scientific research will produce a flash equal to the power of 100,000 nuclear power plants. But it will last less than a millionth of a second.

▶ FUTURE TREND

WALKING THROUGH WALLS?
All objects are made of atoms. Atoms are tiny and very far apart, even in solid materials, such as wood or metal. So all objects are mostly empty space inside. The maser can make atoms resonate, or shake, at a certain speed. At exactly the right resonance, could the resonating atoms of one object pass between the atoms of another? If they could, you could walk through a wall.

LASERS IN THE FUTURE

Every year there are more lasers, more types of lasers, and more uses for lasers. Besides laser versions of existing machines, there could be completely new devices. How about a laser-sniffer that identifies a million different scents and smells? Or a laser fence that keeps unwanted people and animals out—or in?

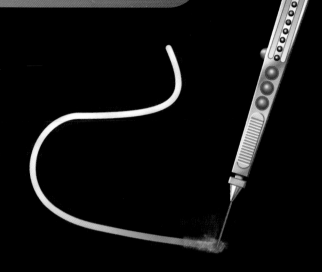

A laser knife could slice through a book, wood, or metal as easily as a real knife through soft butter.

LASER COMMUNICATIONS

The **Information Revolution** is based on lasers. CDs and hologram memories hold more and more information. Optical fiber cables carry information faster and farther around the telecommunications network. It's the electrical parts of the system, such as local phone lines, that slow it down. If the whole network were optical, based on pulses of laser light, it could be 100 times more efficient.

LASER COMPUTERS

The computers we use now are electronic. But an optical computer could be 1,000 times more powerful than today's PC (personal computer). It would use flashes of laser light and would carry more information, more quickly. But much research is still needed into switches and components that work by light rather than by electricity.

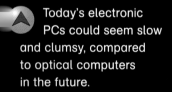
Today's electronic PCs could seem slow and clumsy, compared to optical computers in the future.

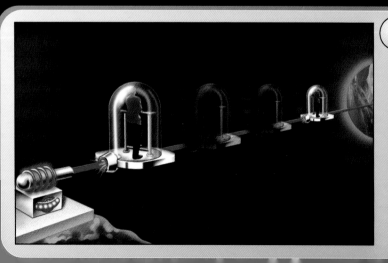

▶ **FUTURE TREND**

CATCHING THE WAVE?

As light waves hit an object, they give out a tiny pushing force in the direction they are traveling. In daily life this force is far too small to notice. But scientists have used powerful lasers to push single atoms and other tiny particles. In the distant future a mega-powerful laser could move larger objects. Like a surfer riding the ocean waves, you could be pushed along at the front of a laser beam and travel from here to there in the blink of an eye.

THE LASER TOOTH DRILL

A visit to the dentist may never be the same again. Dental lasers can now bore holes in teeth to remove decay without the pain of a drill. The first versions of these dental lasers did not work properly. In fact, they made teeth explode. Luckily

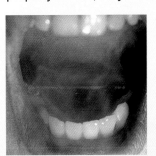

they were being tested on people who had died and left their bodies for medical research. Lasers could help in many other areas of medicine, too, even bringing an end to surgical operations.

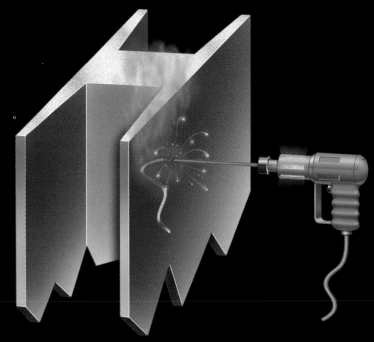

A laser drill could bore through hard metal—and make square holes too!

LASER MACHINES

As lasers become smaller, cheaper, and more powerful, they could be built into many tools and devices. We could have laser drills, laser saws, laser knives, laser hammers, and, far more dangerously, laser ray guns. The concentrated energy of lasers could also be used to control chemical changes and even nuclear reactions. This could help to prevent nuclear disasters, reduce **radioactive** pollution, and provide cleaner, safer power far into the future.

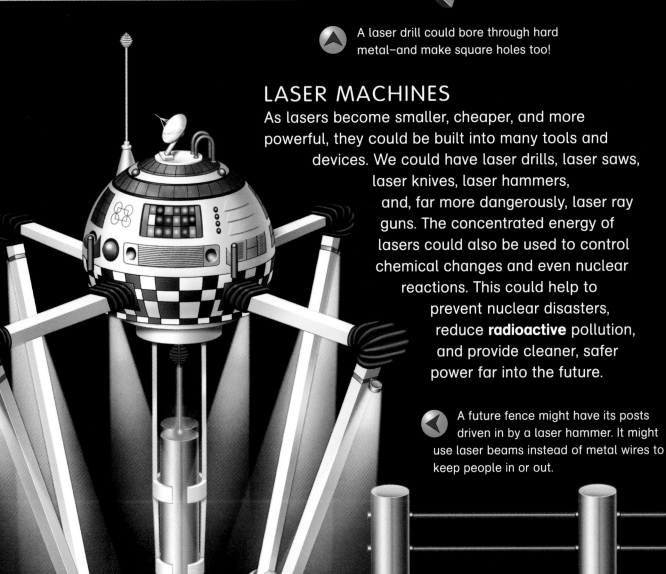

A future fence might have its posts driven in by a laser hammer. It might use laser beams instead of metal wires to keep people in or out.

GLOSSARY

active medium The substance a laser is made from. The active medium can be a liquid or gas, or a gem, such as ruby. The active medium becomes excited, or stimulated by energy, and gives off flashes of light.

atoms Tiny particles–too small to be seen–that make up all objects and matter, including our bodies.

axle A rod, pole, or shaft through the center of a wheel, pulley, or similar spinning device.

bearings Devices in machines where one part spins around or moves against another part, such as a wheel or axle. Bearings are usually used with oil and are designed to give easy, smooth movement.

big bang When the universe and everything in it began and started to spread out, with a gigantic explosion. Scientists think that this probably happened about 12 to 14 billion years ago.

blood vessels The network of tubes that carry blood all around the body.

coherence When light, or other kinds of waves, are exactly in step, with their peaks and troughs lined up.

distorted Changed and made unclear in some way, such as being bent, blurred, or fuzzy.

electronic component A part or device that works using tiny pulses of electricity.

endoscope A telescope-like tube that is put into the body for medical reasons. It might be put down the throat or through a cut in the skin. Doctors can look through an endoscope into the body, and its tip may have small tweezers, hooks, or similar parts.

fiber optic A thin, hair-like strand, or fiber, made of clear glass or plastic, which carries pulses of light along its length. (Optics is the science of light.)

filter A device that lets certain things pass through but stops others. For example, a colored filter lets only light waves of a certain color through and stops all the other colors.

focus When light rays are bent so that they come together into one point. Usually, focusing is done by a curved piece of glass or plastic, called a lens.

image scanner A machine that detects a picture, or image, in a series of very thin lines. It usually converts the shapes, patterns, and colors in the image into coded electrical signals, to feed into a computer or printer.

Information Revolution The fast-changing ways in which we can receive more information about more topics, faster and more easily–especially by using computers linked by the telephone network, as in the Internet.

infrared Rays or waves that are part of the electromagnetic spectrum or EMS. They are similar to visible light rays, but their waves are longer. We cannot see infrared rays, but we can feel them as they have a warming or heating effect.

integrated circuit A group of electronic components usually on a chip of silicon. Also called microchip.

laser scalpel A device that uses a laser beam to cut very accurately. Laser scalpels are used widely in medicine to make fine cuts into body parts.

lens A piece of clear glass or plastic with curved sides, which bends light rays as they shine through it. The human eye has a natural lens that does this, so that we can see clearly.

light waves Rays or waves that are part of the electromagnetic spectrum, or EMS. Light rays can be detected by our eyes.

microchip See **integrated circuit**.

microcircuit The tiny, or microscopic, sets of electronic components on a microchip.

microwaves Rays or waves that are part of the electromagnetic spectrum, or EMS. We cannot see microwaves, but we can use them to make heat.

molten The condition of a solid substance, such as rock or metal, that becomes liquid when heated.

nuclear Involving the nucleus, the central part of an atom. (See **atom**.) Nuclear power is produced by splitting an atom apart.

optical Using or working by light. Optics is the science of light.

pit A hole or scooped-out shape.

prism A block of clear material, such as glass, with flat, angled sides, which can split, bend, or reflect light rays.

pulse A short burst of something, like a flash of light, a surge of electricity, or a short, sharp sound.

radiation Any form of energy that is given out, or radiated, from a source as rays, waves, or particles.

radioactive Giving off certain kinds of energy as invisible rays that can harm living things.

refraction The bending or turning of light at an angle as it passes from one substance to another, such as from air to glass, or from air to water.

semiconductor A substance that *partly* carries, or conducts, electricity (this is why it is called a *semi*conductor). The main semiconductor is silicon, used in microchips, or integrated circuits.

sensor A device or machine that senses, detects, or receives something, usually producing electrical signals. Our eyes are living light sensors.

silicon A brownish substance, or chemical element, which can be dug from the ground, purified, and made into crystals. The crystals are then sliced into waferlike microchips that carry electricity.

stimulated emission The giving out of energy when stimulated, or excited, by another energy source.

telecommunications Sending, receiving, or communicating information over long distances, such as between computers or telephones. Telecommunications systems use metal wires, fiber-optic cables, radio signals, satellite links, and other methods.

tissue The many different substances, microscopic cells, and materials that make up our bodies.

vaporize To change a solid or liquid into a vapor, usually by heating it. The vapor is like gas or smoke and drifts away into the air.

virtual reality An object, scene, landscape, or something similar that seems real to our senses, but is not because it is created by a computer.

watt A unit for measuring the power, or strength, of electricity and other forms of energy.

wavelength The length of one complete wave, such as a light or sound wave, from one tip or peak to the next tip or peak.

weld To join two parts by making them so hot that they melt together, or fuse. The materials then become solid again to form one single part. Welding is usually done with metals.

INDEX